SONGS OF WAKING

Songs of Waking

JONATHAN SIMONS

SONGS OF WAKING
Copyright © 2016 by Jonathan Sklar Simons

All rights reserved. Printed in the Netherlands. No part of this book may be used or reproduced in any manner whatsoever without written permission from the author except in the case of brief quotations embodied in critical articles and reviews.

Published by Analog Sea
PO Box 11670
Austin, Texas 78711
United States

FIRST EDITION

Library of Congress Control Number: 2015917630

ISBN 978-0-692-56233-8

Contents

Small Fire	1
In the Night	2
Madrid	3
Driftwood	5
Hungry Ghost	7
Salt Spring Island	9
On Forgetting	12
Polaris	15
Castaways	17
From the Shore	19
Moving Closer	20
The Factory	21
Midnight Sun	23
The Seamstress	25
When the Sun Sighs	26
Golden	28
Like a Soldier	30
The Butterfly	32
Solid Ground	33
Shelter	34
A Thousand Empty Rooms	37

Solitude	38
Currency	40
Mirage	42
Thirst	44
Upon the Banks of That River	45
Song from the Void	47
Tracks	48
When the Last Bell Tolls	49
Sensation of a Moment	52
Life on the Wing	53

SONGS OF WAKING

Small Fire

How to stay awake
when the walls are shaking,
when even stars burn white holes
through the curtain
as I fall deeper into sleep.

How to raise a fist
from these heavy arms
and a body
no longer pulled
by taut sails of youth.

How to carry the small fire,
that little inferno, hope —
the fruit tree,
its black shade,
its branches reaching outward,
its dreams —
when the trains are always
running late.

In the Night

The lamplighter,
his footsteps, his golden bow,
wakes you from a dream.

Your heart plays
a somber rhythm,
gathering kindling in the yard.

The sparrow pecks at your ear.
The fire, soon ash and soot,
brings you morning.

What will you do
with this feast of energy,
this life of longing and decay?

What will you do
with the promises
you make in the light?

Madrid

In Madrid
the old farmers
carry big spools
of electric wire.

In Sevilla
the stone horses run
but only in streets
where barefoot boys dream.

Where is Spanish soil
in this swollen metropolis?

Where is the afternoon sun,
its timeless swinging in the yard,
when the skies of Barcelona
are eclipsed
by steel salutes
to London,
to Shanghai?

Where is the vertical dream,
patterns the feet make
in the clay,

the love of red earth
looking back at you
like the eyes of Marina.

Driftwood

Along these medieval steps,
antiquity moans
her familiar songs
of death.

The city on the hill,
its marble promise
hung upon the same
steeple spire.

And so too is it written
on that stiff flag
puncturing the dusty flesh
of the moon.

There are lighthouses
dotting the seas;
those flickering bulbs
burn the horizon,
burn up the golden braid,
burn up the dreams
we carry as children,
as uninitiated visitors
of fallout shelters.

Arms wide to the shore,
we are driftwood,
eager explorers
of hope and fear.

Hungry Ghost

I see your trembling heart
growing weary
from battle.

Lies you pick
from fields
of loud voices,
as clay before a cup
of water,
as a child
before her first sea.

Like the mind
of the executioner
dying into a grave
already full,
you spend your days
searching beehives
for honey.

Like a beggar,
your outstretched hands
cursing the moon,
the nights you spend

scouring anthills
for a queen.

Can't you see
the whale
parting the ocean?

Can't you see
the lion
growing its mane?

And the city coughs.
And the crow
brings you blackness.
And the mountain,
little, white flakes
of snow.

Salt Spring Island

Among the icy limbs
of trees,
a voice,
a silver echo crosses
the frozen pond.

Between stiff but swaying
towers rising from city centers,
a man lays down his hands
beside two lit candles
placed on the oak table.

We, the dreamers,
the living-living and living-dead,
have already lost our game.

We, the ghosts of flesh,
our hearts beating
their many reveries of nothingness,
have surely died;
our dreams of youth awoken
by the lucid sonority
of church bells
crashing in the yard.

Ripped from the flight
of white immersion,
we are the yard birds,
our lullabies fading,
our naked bodies cribbed
in metallic rhythms
of a million trains
travelling nowhere,
directed only by the speed
of running
from something
too soft to hold
within the icy arms of trade.

We, the child soldiers,
our mother's shelter
becoming rifles and swords
in the night,
our poems replaced
with madness while we sleep.

We, the dreamers,
the living-living and living-dead,
have already lost our game.

But the marrow
still boils in the bone,
the ocean still pulses
through soft chambers
of the heart,
our constellatory minds
carry still
those ancient maps of stars,
a compass of beauty
not yet sold
at the garden's gate —

Should an old bottle wash up
with the message
once scribbled with urgency of youth.

Should a small key fall
from behind
the forgotten photograph.

On Forgetting

Time
and time again,
I see tree,

not wind
threaded and wound
through leaves
by autumn.

I see people,
but not
as lighthouses
for waking.

Time
and time again,
I forget magic.

I see a world
of want, need, not
drumbeats of longing.

I see a city
heavied by coins

and not
her summer dress
floating on the line.

Time
and time again,
I forget space.

I see rooms
and halls,
not contours
of dreaming.

I see bees
and hives,
not honey
becoming.

Time
and time again,
I forget time.

I see night
as a black tarp,

not as practice
for dying.

I see trains
and highways,
but not swallows
bringing spring.

Time
and time again,

I forget
the swiftness
of dusk.

Polaris

There is a woman
in a room,
her white dress
pushed and pulled
by the ocean.

The moon stains her arms gray
as she stands perched
in the window frame,
waiting for what,
I'll never know.
More night?
Some sort of midnight eclipse?
A black illumination?

Morning will shake me again,
back to chasing those balloons
I lost as a child,
so early burned
by that Texas sun,
dreaming in the desert,
never having slept in forest
or at sea.

So yes, I am a balloon chaser,
my pockets full of seeds
and photographs,
maps of the Persian Sea,
of Berlin,
nautical charts,
sketches from a dream I had
of the Northern Lights.

Castaways

How will this trip be for you,
your shift from flesh,
from wet lips pressed
into me,
from invisible snares,
taut and waiting,
from two rippling animals,
clumsy arms stretched and clawing
for a little smoke,
our eyes clouded by
forever
and always,
and yes
and no
and never,
from across this razor's edge
of touch,
without face, without oils of skin,
without skin,
your shift from flesh
to memory.

Castaways,
we swim toward separate shores.

We flounder
before a laughing moon
and heavy our wings with oil.

Before the gush of morning
floods you,
before your porous skin
meets the salt of your flight,
lay your dreams upon my body.

From the Shore

Show me your eyes,
your trophies
from swimming
some great sea.

Some great sea
you swam,
through winter and spring,
through the brush
of a mind
you no longer recognize.

You no longer recognize
the curves and lines
you see in the mirror,
nor that placid face
staring back at you
in the night.

In the night
you stare death
a little more
in the eye.

Moving Closer

I am moving closer
to blood that shaped me,
blood that spilled
with me in mind.

I am moving closer
to spirits
that know me
by silent names.

I am moving closer
to a threshold
where I become them
and time is but a story
to tell on some train.

The Factory

From this heap of arrows
I fire
wood and flint
into darkness.

At night I dream
of caves and wells.

I am a jay
flying downward
through some secret vein,
some uncharted conduit
of blackness and rock,
down toward a fiery center
where the blueprint itself
is consumed.

At night I dream
again and again
of my childhood body,
those small hands
reaching outward,
conducting smoke

before an orchestra
of burning embers.

Young eyes.
Young meditative eyes,
transfixed by flames
and dreams
of becoming a man.

Midnight Sun

A friend has died.
I hang up the phone,
straighten some books
and a few drops of spilt tea
from the desk.

I take a photo from the shelf.
I think of whom to call
to share a little death
with the living.

When his body hits the earth,
will it wake me?
Will we see our shadows
through the haze and glare
of the midnight sun?

And when we pay the priest,
will the dead return?
Will we remove our childhoods
from our leather bags
and run through the streets
with flowers spilling from our hair?

I wash the dishes
and stare at winter
through the glass.

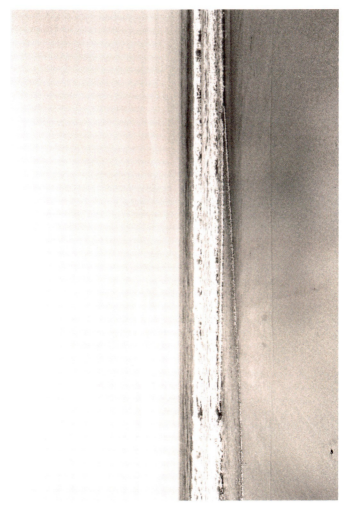

Analog Sea

Dear Reader,

So you managed to find us amid all the flickering and noise. Thank you for that, and for supporting your local bookstores and record stores.

If you discover something valuable in this work, please tell other daydreamers about Analog Sea, our books and music, and our wish for a little slowness now and then.

And if you want to stay in touch, to receive our newsletter and other mailings, why not send us a letter? Be sure to include your name, mailing address, and perhaps what was happening when you first discovered the Analog Sea.

Poems, drawings, recordings, and other outpourings of solitude are always welcome.

Yours truly,
Analog Sea

Basler Str. 115
79115 Freiburg
Germany

PO Box 11670
Austin, TX 78711
United States

The Seamstress

Are we not all like
the seamstress,
cutting out felt stars
from cardboard guides,
walking the cobble
like ghosts of another time,
our hands translucent
and powerless,
our hearts beating
in rhythm
to the new machines.

Sing me a song of mediocrity.
Illuminate this withering body;
wash out its shadows,
its oaken lines, its black and blue,
with lights from the city.

Sing me a song of the desert.
Open the stiff curtain;
flood my dreams with whiteness.
Drain this ocean I carry
and give me mirages of sea,
patterns of a woman I follow in the sand.

When the Sun Sighs

When the sun sighs
and darkness finds you
in the steps,
do you hear
the blind poets of Paris
singing those old
songs of love?

The lamppost,
stiff and solitary
like your own
teetering body,
brings you shadows
of the Belle Époque,
muted glimmers
from elder eyes
you meet in the street.

And if you threw yourself
into the Seine,
what would you find
there, in the depths,
in the folds of promises

once lit by lamplight,
whispers made in the crossing?

All of this
you see in the faces
of old Parisians,
in the brick and brass
and reflections you catch
in the glass.

And if you found yourself,
once and for all, caressed
by untouchable waters,
what would you find there,
among the sunken promises,
among the skin of old youth,
among the refuse of love?

Golden

Was it not good enough
crawling on all fours,
the sky full of stars,
shards of amazement
shooting through
that new body?

Was I not fast enough,
cruising the yard
on a broomstick saddle,
Rodeo Junior cowboy hat
and Pop's paper
tucked up my sleeve?

Did I not fly for you?
Did I not point,
wide-eyed and staring,
at those moons of fire?

Did I not love for you?
Did I not hold you quivering
in the unlit hall
before you took the light

and your black bag
from the stair?

Was I not golden?
Did I not shimmer?
Did I not resist
your long arms
pushing me out
into a world
of shadows?

Like a Soldier

Like a soldier
tying up
his big black boot,
you crawl your way
into the machine.

And with the click
of the clock tower
you assemble,
to peck out
little digits from time.

Like that polished latch
that closes you,
you spend your days
piecing together
a broken egg.

But where is dusk for you?
Where is the night
when the torches of need
burn up the feminine,
burn up the dark cloak
covering night?

Your life is a drain
through which you flush
all the little things.

But the morning brings you
stillness,
your eyes still wet
with memory
of where you're going.

The Butterfly

The butterfly
whispers nothingness
into forgetful ears.

The flapping of wings
points me onward,
my journey closer
to the great ballroom,
my original home.

Solid Ground

She is a mirage,
a reflection of the poems
you write in the night.

She is a little patch
of green
you find, lost
in the deep sea.

She is a flamenco guitar
tossing salt and wine
at a funeral.

In her shadow,
your dreams become
ladders or dust.

And along her skin
you stretch
minutes to hours,
where the willow's tired arms
fall gently upon
solid ground.

Shelter

How could I save
even one of them,
before the great wheel
sweeps them up, limb by limb,
before those supple branches
become more stiff posts
lighting the lanes
of commerce?

How could I shelter
even one,
keeping that spark lit
with forest kindling,
that buoyancy of heart
from the weight of becoming,
the weight of money?

How could I ever lift
even one of them
high enough to see
over hunchbacked shoulders
of the crowd,
onward, past rows
of deserted gardens,

across oceans
toward lighthouses flickering,
onward still,
to funnels of smoke rising
from funeral pyres
in the distance?

I spend my nights
carving these glyphs
into your wall,
polishing old relics,
a compass to leave
at your door.

My days building bridges
to carry you
between dreams.

Yet your thirst
for dark water.
Yet your grandmother's
rings of ruby,
your father's stern gaze
and the tears you save

from your mother.

Yet that dusk in autumn,
its amber borders
you see now
through tinted glass,
your toes now skimming
abysmal waters,
your eyelids
soon heavy
from dreaming.

A Thousand Empty Rooms

I carry my body
in and around
many rooms,
most of them
much quieter
than this nervous
chatter within.

The drapes sway,
moved slowly and gently
by summer,
reflecting tapestries
of light, hovering
between a falling sun
and four white walls.

And when,
in one of a thousand empty rooms,
I find my equal in space,
the peace pours into me
like quiet torrents through a keyhole.

Solitude

Solitude,
my bedfellow,
that stretch of bone
supporting a beating heart,
a beating drum from falling
to oceanic graves, the crowd.

You know my death so well
and whisper its song
constantly in my ear.

Are you not the last casket into which
I one day so wearily crawl,
before the smaller box
is fitted and ordered from the store?

Are you not that pillar I leaned upon
through those long, epic nights
after the iron oar
fell and struck?

I remember ancient arms
pulling me in
like moss on redwood.

But the city grows loud and stiff.
Soon the floors shake.
Soon enough you see the bombs
falling, once the white lace
has been drawn,
or ripped down,
from the sill.

Then a voice in the night asks
how to find that trail of crumbs,
all those little arrows
leading back to the forest,
back to that silent room
where we empty ourselves of time.

Should we lose each other once again
I hope to find you by the stream,
or beneath the bending arms
of the willow tree.

I hope to find you riding
the wild winds of autumn
or in the long darkness of winter.

Currency

There is a currency I carry,
mostly coins of beauty,
coins of death.

I wear a uniform,
a woolen coat keeps the skin
from burning.

A few old medals
remind me of lost treasure,
pockets once full of seashells
and arrowheads.

Now I'm grown and tower
a little closer to the sun,
my legs trace circles
in the sand,
in search of a center,
where I might stop,
where I might catch the clock
falling from the wall,
where an image stretches out
before me, white
upon a black screen,

a silhouette of a boy
discovering stillness
before the edge
of a great ocean.

Mirage

A thousand stories burn
through subway tunnels
like stars,
brilliant and consumed
by fire
and mythology
and the longing of lovers
divided by parting trains.

So too
my body carries
a thousand stories,
of sadness,
of joy,
of a man walking
through dusk
in search of a lost taste,
a forgotten spice
not grown
in foreign soil.

From time to time
a mirage of home appears
reflected on the wall,

a shadow of mother
revealed in your eyes
as they open from a long sleep,
an undiscovered constellation
beaming down
from a black canvas,
those stars becoming arrows
of fire
shooting across the horizon,
impressions of light remaining
under closed eyes
as I dream.

Thirst

Because all you know
is thirst,
because you pledge allegiance
to yourself,
because your tomahawk
is sheathed
in silk and feather,

because your heart
is just a muscle,
because you shoot
from the hip,
because your smile
consumes you,

you will find me enlisted,
drunk on my vow,
parading the front
with my little flag,
warning the others,
extracting the hook.

Upon the Banks of That River

Your eyes,
heavy and sinking,
find patterns
in the cobble.

The gray dust
of suffering
brings new hues to stars
left on the crown.

It's the mind
always wanting
something
other
than
this.

What are we to do,
the creator gods,
our brushes broken,
our colors left drying
upon the banks of that river?

Are we not like the golden child,
the golden-eyed apprentice,
sentenced to a lifetime observing
some other woman's work?

The candle burns quickly;
your majesty expires
and you are once again
that swelling moan
falling from the cracking egg.

Where is love for you?
A dim light shining
in the wilderness?

Your random wanderings
are marbles falling
from your coat pocket.

Song from the Void

I play my melody,
a grand parade
of little nothingnesses,
for you.

I play a lamenting lute,
a lost compass
left rusting
upon the iron gate.

For you, I sing a song
from the void.

A heartbeat fills the room.
A sunbeam,
a window,
a wall,
a candle burning
at two ends,
a great solitude.

Tracks

Where do we go from here,
this centrifuge of circles,
this desert wind erasing
tracks we make in the night;

this, the midday sun,
neither rising nor falling,
neither compass nor oracle
shouting out the way;

this, the new frontier
where vulture and you
wait together,
where whiteness erodes
the scripture
scraped into the tablet;

this, the projector spinning
in reverse,
Sisyphus staring down at you,
proud and leaning
against some boulder
like a hero.

When the Last Bell Tolls

When the last bell tolls
and falls completely from the tower
in which a lifetime was spent
polishing brass,
sweeping golden shavings
from planks and beams
and watching the sun—
those golden arms tracing
a westward journey,
reflecting first
that fragile outer rim,
then slowly, the strong
bell interior,
and out again,
at last retreating
into the wood,
the sand,
the waves,
and disappearing.

When the last bell tolls
and falls
completely from the tower
in which a lifetime was spent

maintaining its suspension,
keeping soft its swing,
striking only with the precision
of daybreak.

When the last bell tolls
and falls
completely from the tower,
who will deliver the message
that the hour has come
for the farmer
to fall back into soil,
for the market clerk
to remember
the value
of invisible goods,
for the rabbi
to place his moist lips
upon the wall?

When the last bell tolls
and falls
completely
from the tower,

may both the bell and I
stand regal,
trembling to the core,
until the swelling howl
brings us swiftly
to that great void.

Sensation of a Moment

Like a child bending
to inspect a small stone,
I do the one thing
over and over again
that never matters.

Life on the Wing

Will that last morning
wake me with birdsong?
Will the window even be open
so my soul may swim
(or glide) toward that life
on the wing?

And what will I have to offer
those invisible gates?
What could a sparrow possibly sing
before that great silence?

I must not waste time
staring dumbfounded
at the chisel left here in the night;
for tearing down walls,
for opening long darkened caves,
for exposing the only utterance,
the only light remaining
after death's great fire.

And when the poem
has faded from the page,

I draw the cord
and close the shop

hoping I noticed
the graceful dancer
in your step,
that sudden flash
of space
before the word,
hoping I served you well,
dear friend.